PEER MEDIATION

Conflict Resolution in Schools

STUDENT MANUAL

Fred Schrumpf
Donna Crawford
H. Chu Usadel

Research Press Company
2612 North Mattis Avenue
Champaign, Illinois 61821

Cover design by Jack W. Davis
Composition by Wadley Graphix Corporation
Printed by Malloy Lithographing

ISBN 0–87822–331–2
Library of Congress Catalog No. 91–62575

Contents

Training Activities

Peer Mediation Forms

Training Activities

Congratulations on being selected a peer mediator.

You were selected because—

▲ Your teachers felt you have the **qualities** necessary to be a skilled mediator.

▲ You have **good judgment** and the **respect** of your peers. You are probably a person other students can talk to and **trust**.

▲ You represent one of the various groups that make up the school. As you know, every school has a variety of people, personalities, cultures, and ethnic groups. We want you to speak from your **personal experience** and for the peers you represent.

In this training workshop, we want to build on your positive qualities and abilities. We will teach you how to help students who are in conflict work together to solve their own problems. This process of conflict resolution is called **peer mediation**.

Specifically, you will learn—

▲ The causes and results of conflict

▲ The role of the mediator

▲ Communication skills

▲ Steps in the mediation process

The workshop is experiential, which means you will learn by doing. Everyone will have a chance to share ideas and experiences about conflict and to practice peer mediation situations. This training is an opportunity to increase your knowledge of conflict, learn the skills of conflict resolution, and have fun.

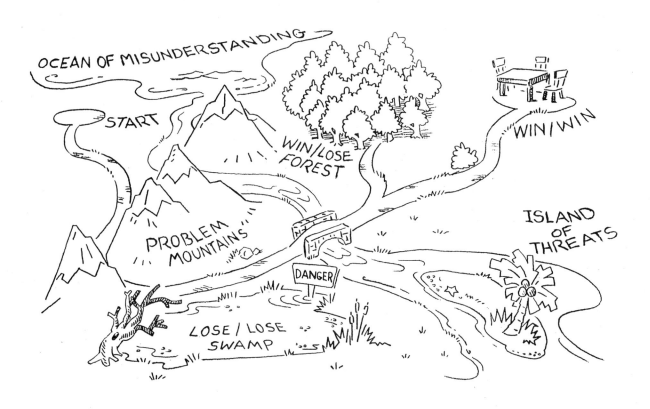

PEER MEDIATION: DEFINITION AND GOALS

Mediation is an approach to resolve conflict in which the **disputants**, or the people who disagree, have the chance to sit face to face and talk uninterrupted so each side of the dispute is heard. After the problem is defined, solutions are created and then evaluated. When an agreement is reached, it is written and signed.

The **goals** of peer mediation are as follows.

▲ For disputants to understand and respect different views

▲ To open and improve communication

▲ To develop cooperation in solving a common problem

▲ To reach agreements that address the interests of both sides

When one person wins and another loses in a dispute, we say it is a **win/lose situation**. Sometimes both people can lose in a conflict situation, as is the case when someone works so hard to hurt the other person that he or she also gets hurt. We call this a **lose/lose situation**. Peer mediation is a **win/win approach** to conflict: Both people are winners, and no one loses.

ROLE OF THE PEER MEDIATOR

A trained peer mediator is a neutral third person who leads the mediation process. The mediator helps the disputants communicate and keeps all information **confidential**. This means not discussing the disputants' problem with other students in the school. Peer mediators—

▲ Are the peacemakers for the school

▲ Listen to and respect all points of view

▲ Understand their own conflicts and how to handle them

▲ Know how to help other students resolve their conflicts

ASSUMPTIONS OF PEER MEDIATION

It takes cooperation and understanding to resolve conflicts. Peer mediation is based on the belief that, in order to resolve conflicts, people must be willing to do the following.

▲ Stay calm and control their anger

▲ Focus on the problem and not blame the other person

▲ Honestly state their wants and feelings

▲ Understand and respect the other person's point of view

▲ Cooperate and create solutions that meet the needs of everyone involved

STATEMENTS ABOUT CONFLICT

People live, work, and play together, and it is important for them to get along. To do so, people must understand the following ideas about conflict.

▲ Conflict is a natural part of everyday life.

▲ Conflict can be handled in positive or negative ways.

▲ Conflict can have either creative or destructive results.

▲ Conflict can be a positive force for personal growth and social change.

BASIC NEEDS

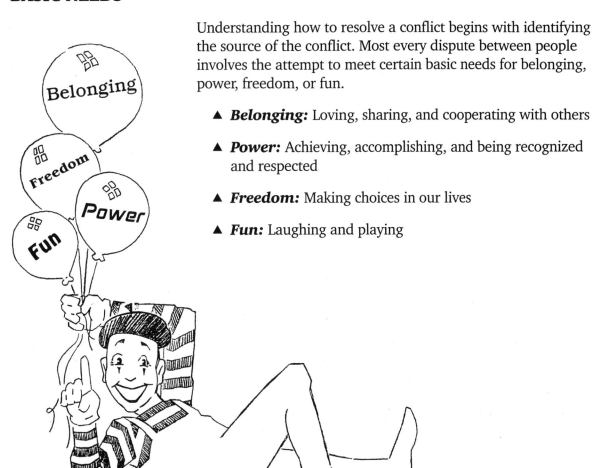

Understanding how to resolve a conflict begins with identifying the source of the conflict. Most every dispute between people involves the attempt to meet certain basic needs for belonging, power, freedom, or fun.

▲ **Belonging:** Loving, sharing, and cooperating with others

▲ **Power:** Achieving, accomplishing, and being recognized and respected

▲ **Freedom:** Making choices in our lives

▲ **Fun:** Laughing and playing

We might think that people or situations cause us to act a certain way, but this belief is not true. We act the way we do because we are trying to meet our basic needs. For instance, suppose you are upset because your friend is going to a party and you were not invited. You might get into a conflict with the friend because you are not getting your need for **belonging** met. Or suppose you are in conflict with a parent about the chores you must do around the house. This conflict might be the result of your need to have the **freedom** to make your own choices about how to spend your time.

LIMITED RESOURCES AND DIFFERENT VALUES

Often limited resources or different values appear to be the underlying cause of conflicts.

Conflicts that involve **limited resources** can be about a lack of time, money, or property. For instance, two classmates are having a conflict over property when they are arguing about who will get to use a certain book they both want for a report.

When people in conflict talk about honesty, equal rights, or fairness, the conflict is probably about **different values**. People have different convictions, priorities, and principles, and these differences can mean conflict. For instance, a student who values honesty in her friends will probably be very upset and angry if a friend lies to her. Conflicts involving values tend to be difficult to resolve because when people's values are different, they often perceive the dispute as a personal attack. Resolving a values conflict does not mean the disputants must change or align their values. Often a mutual acknowledgment that each person views the situation differently is the first step toward resolution.

Unmet needs are at the heart of conflicts over limited resources and different values. We want certain resources (time, money, property) or hold certain values (honesty, fairness, equality) because they satisfy basic needs. Resources and values are **wants**. We choose wants to satisfy our needs.

So, the two classmates fighting over the book they both want for a report are really attempting to get their **power** needs met. If they fail the class or do not write a quality report, they will not be accomplishing or achieving, and they may not be recognized or respected by themselves or others. Likewise, the student who is angry because her friend lied to her is attempting to get her **belonging** need met. She finds it difficult to share and cooperate with someone who is not honest.

RESPONSES TO CONFLICT

People can choose one of three ways of responding to conflict: avoidance, confrontation, or communication.

Avoidance

People avoid conflict by withdrawing from the situation, ignoring the problem, or denying their feelings. Avoiding the conflict may help in the short run—for instance, it might help someone keep from losing his temper. However, avoidance usually makes a person doubt himself or feel anxious about the future. In addition, because the conflict is never brought up, it can never be resolved. As a result, the person's basic needs are never met.

Confrontation

Confrontation in response to conflict means a person expresses anger, verbal or physical threats, or aggression. It may also mean the person resorts to bribery or to punishments like withholding money, favors, or affection. These actions show a win/lose attitude toward conflict. The attitude that one person must win and the other person must lose in a conflict prevents cooperation and keeps people from reaching a mutually satisfying solution.

Communication

Communication in response to conflict means to participate in a common understanding, not necessarily to agree. In order for people to cooperate, they must first communicate. People in conflict who seek first to understand the other person's side, then be understood, produce win/win resolutions. In other words, both people get their needs met, and no one loses.

CONFLICT DIAGRAM

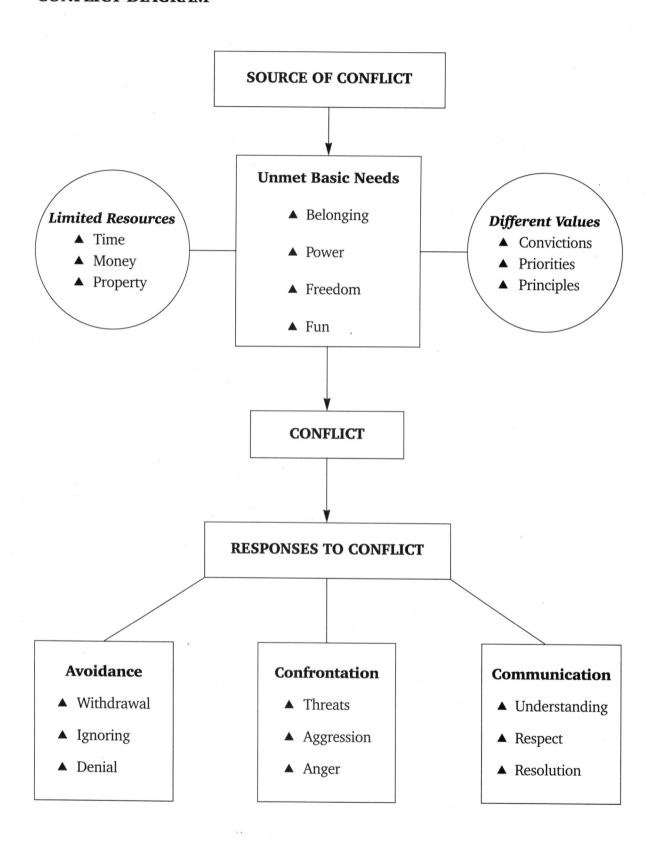

Defining Conflict

PART I

Conflict _____

Conflict _____

Conflict _____

Conflict _____

Conflict _____

PART II

Conflict _____

Conflict _____

Conflict _____

Conflict _____

Conflict _____

Meeting Basic Needs

Directions: Write down the things you do to get your needs met in each of the following areas.

1. **Belonging:** Loving, sharing, and cooperating with others

_____

_____

_____

_____

2. **Power:** Achieving, accomplishing, and being recognized and respected

_____

_____

_____

_____

3. **Freedom:** Making choices in our lives

_____

_____

_____

_____

4. **Fun:** Laughing and playing

_____

_____

_____

_____

Understanding the Source of Conflict

Directions: Describe a recent conflict you had at school.

1. Who was involved?_____

_____

_____

2. How did you feel?_____

_____

_____

3. What did the other person want?_____

_____

_____

4. What did you want?_____

_____

_____

5. Were limited resources or different values involved in the conflict? If so, how?

_____

_____

_____

6. What do you think the unmet basic need or needs were behind the conflict? (Remember, these needs could be for belonging, power, freedom, or fun.)

_____

_____

_____

Identifying Responses to Conflict

Directions: Check whether you think these responses are examples of avoidance, confrontation, or communication. Then circle the numbers of the three responses you most commonly use when in conflict.

1. Ignore the situation

   ☐ avoidance   ☐ confrontation   ☐ communication

2. Threaten the other person

   ☐ avoidance   ☐ confrontation   ☐ communication

3. Fight it out

   ☐ avoidance   ☐ confrontation   ☐ communication

4. Just give in—it doesn't really matter

   ☐ avoidance   ☐ confrontation   ☐ communication

5. Try to discover new possibilities

   ☐ avoidance   ☐ confrontation   ☐ communication

6. Complain until I get my way

   ☐ avoidance   ☐ confrontation   ☐ communication

7. Admit differences

   ☐ avoidance   ☐ confrontation   ☐ communication

8. Admit I am wrong, even if I don't think so

   ☐ avoidance   ☐ confrontation   ☐ communication

9. Change the subject

   ☐ avoidance   ☐ confrontation   ☐ communication

10. Try to understand the other person's point of view

   ☐ avoidance   ☐ confrontation   ☐ communication

4   **Qualities and Role of the Peer Mediator**

1. The peer mediator remains **unbiased**.

   A mediator is neutral and objective, a person who does not take sides.

2. The peer mediator is an **empathic listener**.

   A mediator is skilled at listening with the intent to understand what each disputant thinks and feels.

3. The peer mediator is **respectful**.

   A mediator is able to treat both parties with respect and understanding, and without prejudice.

4. The peer mediator **helps people work together**.

   A mediator is responsible for the process, not the solutions. When both parties cooperate, they are able to find their own solutions.

5. The peer mediator **keeps information confidential**.

   A mediator builds the disputants' confidence and trust in the process by not discussing their problem with others in the school.

Statements About Me

Directions: Complete the statements by writing the first response that comes to mind.

1. My friends say that I _____

2. I sometimes wish _____

3. I feel best when _____

4. One way I relax is _____

5. I get frustrated with _____

6. In school I _____

7. I feel disappointed when _____

8. I am good at _____

9. My parents expect _____

10. Two words that describe me are _____

11. When I get angry I _____

12. When I trust someone I _____

13. I think a friend is _____

14. I know prejudice can _____

15. I will be an effective peer mediator because _____

Communication occurs when a listener hears and understands a speaker's essential thoughts, acts, and feelings. Many conflicts continue because of poor communication between people. In order to communicate, the peer mediator uses the following specific communication skills: active listening, summarizing, and clarifying.

ACTIVE LISTENING

Active listening means using **nonverbal behaviors** to show you hear and understand. These nonverbal behaviors include tone of voice, eye contact, facial expressions, posture, and gestures. If you are leaning forward, smiling, nodding your head, and ignoring outside distractions, you are actively listening.

SUMMARIZING

Summarizing means you do two things. First, you **restate facts** by repeating the most important points, organizing interests, and discarding extra information. Second, you **reflect feelings** about the conflict. It is very important when summarizing to recognize feelings in the situation as well as facts.

CLARIFYING

Clarifying means using **open-ended questions or statements** to get additional information and to make sure you understand. Some examples of open-ended questions include—

▲ How did you feel about that? (question)

▲ Tell me what happened next in the situation. (statement)

▲ What do you think is keeping you from reaching an agreement about this problem? (question)

Open-ended questions can be answered in many different ways and help keep people talking. Closed questions can only be answered yes or no, and closed statements do not really require any response at all. Closed questions and statements such as the following tend to discourage people from further discussion.

▲ Did you feel angry when that happened? (yes-or-no question)

▲ You've been fighting for a long time. (no response needed)

▲ Do you think you can reach an agreement about this problem? (yes-or-no question)

COMMUNICATION PITFALLS

In addition to using closed questions or statements, here are some sure-fire ways a peer mediator can shut down communication.

▲ Interrupt   ▲ Laugh or ridicule

▲ Offer advice   ▲ Criticize

▲ Judge   ▲ Bring up your own experience

Be sure to avoid these common pitfalls!

COMMUNICATION SKILLS DIAGRAM

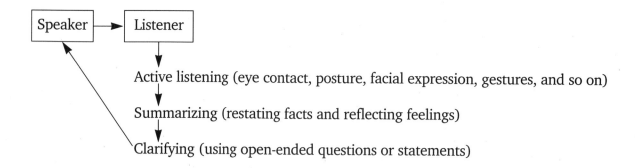

Speaker → Listener

Active listening (eye contact, posture, facial expression, gestures, and so on)

Summarizing (restating facts and reflecting feelings)

Clarifying (using open-ended questions or statements)

Are You An Effective Communicator?

Directions: Use this checklist to evaluate your communication skills.

	Yes	No	Sometimes
1. Do you make eye contact?	☐	☐	☐
2. Do you watch the person's body posture and facial expressions?	☐	☐	☐
3. Do you empathize and try to understand feelings, thoughts, and actions?	☐	☐	☐
4. Do you keep from interrupting and let the person finish, even though you already know what the person means?	☐	☐	☐
5. Do you ask questions to clarify information?	☐	☐	☐
6. Do you smile and nod your head to show interest?	☐	☐	☐
7. Do you listen, even if you do not like the person who is talking or what the person is saying?	☐	☐	☐
8. Do you ignore outside distractions?	☐	☐	☐
9. Do you listen for and remember important points?	☐	☐	☐
10. Do you keep from judging what was said— do you remain neutral?	☐	☐	☐

STEPS IN PEER MEDIATION

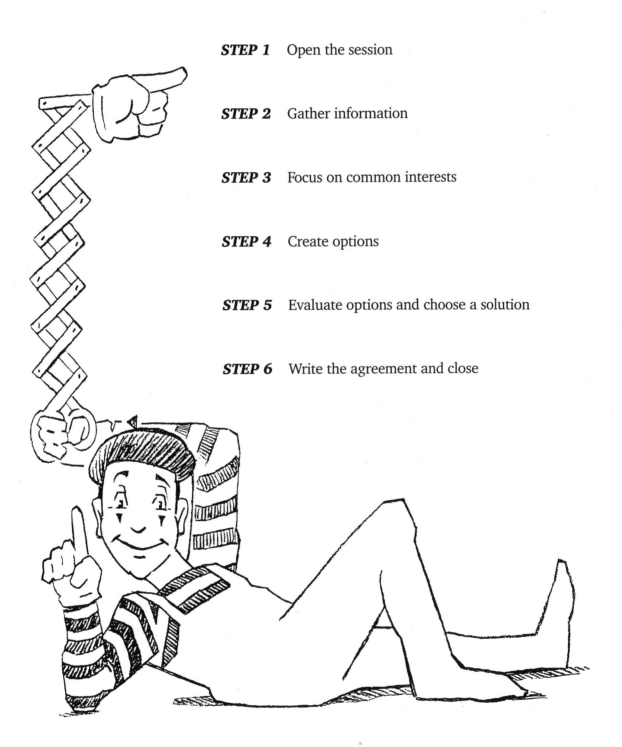

STEP 1   Open the session

STEP 2   Gather information

STEP 3   Focus on common interests

STEP 4   Create options

STEP 5   Evaluate options and choose a solution

STEP 6   Write the agreement and close

CASE EXAMPLE

The following case example shows how a peer mediator used the six steps to help two students reach an agreement. In this situation, Michael and Sondra were referred to the mediation center by the school principal, Mr. Thomas.

STEP 1: Open the session

Mediator: Hello, my name is _____ and I am the mediator assigned to hold this session today. Michael and Sondra, I welcome you both to the mediation center. Let me explain the ground rules. First, I remain neutral—I do not take sides. Everything said in mediation is kept confidential. That means what is said in mediation is not discussed outside this room. Each person takes turns talking without interruption. You are expected to do your best to reach an agreement that considers both your interests. Sondra, do you agree to the rules?

Sondra: Yes.

Mediator: Michael, do you agree to the rules?

Michael: Yeah.

STEP 2: Gather information

Mediator: Sondra, tell me what happened.

Sondra: Michael and I were arguing in the hallway. I got mad and threw my books at him. Then he shoved me against the lockers and was yelling at me when Mr. Thomas saw us. Mr. Thomas suspended Michael. I never fight with anyone—I just got so frustrated with Michael, I lost control.

Mediator: You were frustrated and threw your books at Michael. Mr. Thomas saw Michael shove you and suspended him. What did you think when that happened?

Sondra: I felt bad that Michael got in trouble because I started the fight. We aren't talking, and nothing I do seems to help.

Mediator: Sondra, you're sorry Michael was suspended and you're still frustrated. Michael, tell me what happened.

Michael: Sondra is always getting mad at me. She tells everyone on the tennis team I'm rude and selfish. I missed a practice, and she turns it into a war.

Sondra: You're irresponsible. You're either late for practice or you don't even bother to come.

Mediator: Sondra, it's Michael's turn to talk. Please don't interrupt. Michael, you missed a tennis practice, and Sondra got angry. Tell me more about that.

Michael: Well, we're doubles partners. She takes the game much too seriously. She needs to lighten up. She thinks just because she is my tennis partner, I belong to her. She calls me a lot, but I don't want to be with only one girl all the time. I need my space.

Mediator: Michael, are you saying that you are concerned Sondra wants more from you than just being your tennis partner?

Michael: Yes. She doesn't want me to be with other girls.

Mediator: Sondra, do you have anything else you want to add?

Sondra: Michael takes me for granted. I want him to consider how I feel when he stands me up at practice.

Mediator: Sondra, you want Michael to understand your feelings when he doesn't come to practice and doesn't tell you he won't be there.

Sondra: Yes, that's what I want.

Mediator: Michael, do you have anything to add?

Michael: No.

STEP 3: *Focus on common interests*

Mediator: Sondra, why do you think Michael doesn't tell you when he is not going to make practice?

Sondra: Well . . . he probably doesn't want to hear me yell and cry in front of his friends.

Mediator: Sondra, do you think yelling at Michael will help him get to practice?

Sondra: No, I guess not.

Mediator: Michael, what do you want?

Michael: I want her to stop getting so angry.

Mediator: You don't want Sondra to be mad at you. Michael, if Sondra stood you up for practice, how would you feel?

Michael: Oh, I would be worried she got hurt or something. I probably would be mad if I found out she did it on purpose.

Mediator: You'd be concerned that she was all right and upset if she did it on purpose. Michael, what do you really want?

Michael: What do you mean?

Mediator: Do you want to be Sondra's friend?

Michael: I want to be her friend, and I want to be her tennis partner . . . I don't want to be her boyfriend.

Mediator: You want to be Sondra's friend and tennis partner? Is standing her up for practice helping you get what you want?

Michael: No, it's not helping.

Mediator: Sondra, what do you want?

Sondra: I guess I've wanted Michael to be my boyfriend, and the more I try to make that happen the worse things get.

Mediator: Sondra, can you make Michael be your boyfriend?

Sondra: No, not if he doesn't want to be.

Mediator: Sondra, do you want to be Michael's tennis partner?

Sondra: Yes.

Mediator: Do you want to be his friend?

Sondra: I think so.

STEP 4: Create options

Mediator: It sounds like you both want to be friends and tennis partners. Now, I want you both to think about what you can do to help solve your problems. We'll make a list of possible solutions by brainstorming. The rules for brainstorming are to say any ideas that come to mind, do not judge or discuss the ideas, and look for as many ideas as possible that might satisfy both of you. Ready? What can you do to solve this problem?

Michael: I could stop skipping practice . . .

Sondra: And let me know if you can't make it.

Michael: We could practice before school if we miss a practice . . .

Sondra: I could stop yelling at Michael.

Mediator: What else can you both do to solve the problem?

Michael: We could play tennis on Saturday mornings and then have lunch together.

Sondra: I could stop calling Michael just to talk.

Michael: I could take the tournament that's coming up more seriously . . . I really didn't think it mattered.

Mediator: Can you think of anything else?

Michael: No.

Sondra: No.

STEP 5: *Evaluate options and choose a solution*

Mediator: Which of these ideas will probably work best?

Michael: Well, practicing before school would work.

Sondra: If I don't yell at Michael and stop calling him all the time, he probably would like practice better.

Mediator: Can you do this?

Sondra: If I get upset about something, I could write Michael a note to explain . . . and then we could talk about the problem instead of arguing. Michael could do the same if he's upset about something.

Mediator: Michael, would this work for you?

Michael: It would be better than yelling.

Mediator: What else are you willing to do?

Michael: Well, we have this tournament coming up . . . I would be willing to practice before and after school and on Saturday mornings to make up for the times I've missed.

Mediator: Sondra, are you willing to do that?

Sondra: That practice schedule would be hard work, but I'll do it. I think we can win if we practice real hard. We also need to let each other know if we need to cancel.

Mediator: How would that work?

Michael: We could either call each other or leave notes in each other's lockers.

Mediator: Sondra, do you agree that would help?

Sondra: Yes.

Mediator: You both agree to practice before school, after school, and on Saturdays. What time?

Sondra: How about at 7:30 and 4:00 during the day and at 10:00 on Saturday?

Michael: OK.

Mediator: You both agree to call or leave a note if you need to cancel practice. You both agree if you have a problem in the future you will write a note to explain the problem and then talk to try to work it out.

STEP 6: *Write the agreement and close*

Mediator: (Writes up the agreement, then hands it to Sondra and Michael to sign.) Please look this agreement over to be sure it is correct, then sign it. (Sondra and Michael sign, then the mediator signs. Mediator shakes hands with Sondra, then Michael.) Thank you for participating in mediation. Would you two like to shake hands? (Sondra and Michael shake.)

By preparing properly, you demonstrate a sense of control and establish a secure climate in which the disputants are able to communicate. You prepare for the session by arranging the physical environment and assembling materials.

ARRANGING THE PHYSICAL ENVIRONMENT

Arrange the physical environment in the mediation room so that no one is at any kind of disadvantage. Doing so will help the disputants see you as not taking sides and will help them communicate better.

It is important to decide who will sit where before a mediation session begins and to arrange the chairs before the disputants arrive. In arranging the chairs, follow two guidelines.

▲ Position the disputants face to face across from each other.

▲ Position yourself at the head of the table between the disputants and nearest to the exit.

ASSEMBLING MATERIALS

Before beginning the session, gather the following materials.

▲ Peer Mediation Request

▲ Brainstorming Worksheet

▲ Peer Mediation Agreement

▲ Pens or pencils

Copies of these forms appear at the back of your manual.

An effective opening sets the stage for the rest of the peer mediation session. You open the session by making introductions, stating the ground rules, and getting a commitment to follow the rules.

1. Make introductions.

▲ Introduce yourself.
("I am _____. I am your mediator.")

▲ Ask each disputant for his or her name.

▲ Welcome disputants to the mediation center.

2. State the ground rules.

▲ Mediators remain neutral.
("I am neutral—I do not take sides.")

▲ Mediation is confidential.
("Everything said in mediation is confidential. That means nothing said here will go beyond this room.")

▲ Interruptions are not allowed.
("Each person takes turns talking without interruption.")

▲ Disputants must cooperate.
("You will do your best to reach an agreement that considers both your interests.")

3. Get a commitment to follow the ground rules.
("Do you agree to follow these rules?")

Step 2: Gather Information

In this step, you will use the communication skills of **active listening**, **summarizing**, and **clarifying** to help you understand the disputants' situation and feelings and to help the disputants understand how each perceives the problem. These communication skills are discussed in the reading for Activity 5.

1. Ask each disputant (one at a time) for his or her side of the story.
("Please tell what happened.")

2. Listen, summarize, clarify.

3. Repeat the process by asking for additional information.
("Is there anything you want to add?")

4. Listen, summarize, clarify.

In this step, your goal is to search for interests that join both disputants. **Common interests** serve as the building blocks for an agreement. Unless common interests are identified, disputants probably will not be able to make an agreement they can both keep. Do not move on to Step 4 until you find out what the common interests are.

1. Determine the interests of each disputant by asking one or more of the following questions.

▲ What do you want?

▲ If you were in the other person's shoes, how would you feel? What would you do?

▲ Is *(Example: fighting)* getting you what you want?

▲ What will happen if you do not reach an agreement?

▲ Why has the other disputant not done what you expect?

2. State the common interests by saying something like the following.

▲ Both of you seem to agree that . . .

▲ It sounds like each of you wants . . .

Identifying Common Interests

Directions: Identify the possible positions and common interests the disputants have in the following examples.

Situation	Position	Common Interests
1. Marcus shouts at Tyrone, "You can't apply for the same job I did. There's only one opening, and I was there first!" Tyrone yells, "I deserve that job, too!"		
2. Lisa yells at her sister, Kara, "You can't ride my bike to school anymore. It's never here when I want it!" Kara yells, "I'm riding your bike—you almost never use it!"		
3. Diana is mad at her boyfriend, Jerome, and says, "If you go out with Emma, I'll never speak to you again." Jerome yells back, "Emma is a friend. I'm not her boyfriend!"		
4. James is upset with Malcom: "If you keep asking me for answers in math class, I'll report you to the teacher." Malcom shouts, "Go ahead. I'll report you when you ask me answers in science!"		
5. Keisha says to Natalie, "You can't go on the canoe trip because you can't swim like the rest of us." Natalie cries, "I don't need to swim like you. I'm going anyway!"		

Many possible solutions exist for resolving a conflict. However, when we are upset or frustrated, we often do not consider all of our options. In this step, you will help disputants create, through **brainstorming**, a number of options that could potentially solve their problem.

1. **Explain to disputants that a brainstorming process will be used to find solutions that satisfy both parties.**

2. **State the rules for brainstorming.**

   ▲ Say any ideas that come to mind.

   ▲ Do not judge or discuss the ideas.

   ▲ Come up with as many ideas as possible.

3. **Help the brainstorming process along by using the following questions.**

   ▲ What could be done to resolve this dispute?

   ▲ What other possibilities can you think of?

   ▲ In the future, what could you do differently?

4. **Write the disputants' ideas on a Brainstorming Worksheet.**

12 Step 5: Evaluate Options and Choose a Solution

Your main task in this step is to **help the disputants evaluate and improve on the ideas** they brainstormed in Step 4. It is also important to check the solution to be sure it is sound. If the solution is not sound, you will need to help the disputants work out a better one.

1. ***Ask disputants to nominate ideas or parts of ideas that seem to have the best possibilities of working.***

2. ***Circle these ideas on the Brainstorming Worksheet.***

3. ***Evaluate options circled and invent ways to improve the ideas by using one or more of the following questions.***

   ▲ What are the consequences of deciding to do this?

   ▲ Is this option a fair solution?

   ▲ Does it address the interests of everyone involved?

   ▲ Can it be done?

▲ What do you like best about the idea?

▲ How could you make the idea better?

▲ What if one person did _____?
Could you do _____?

▲ What are you willing to do?

4. When an agreement is reached, check to be sure it is sound by answering the following questions.

▲ Is the agreement **effective?**
(Does the agreement resolve the major concerns and issues each disputant has? Will the agreement help if the problem reoccurs?)

▲ Is the agreement **mutually satisfying?**
(Do both disputants think the agreement is fair?)

▲ Is the agreement **specific?**
(Can you answer who, what, when, where, and how?)

▲ Is the agreement **realistic?**
(Is the plan reasonable? Can it be accomplished?)

▲ Is the agreement **balanced?**
(Does each person agree to be responsible for something?

5. Summarize the agreement.
("You are both agreeing to . . .")

Step 6: Write the Agreement and Close

Writing the agreement at the end of the peer mediation session further clarifies the disputants' responsibility for resolving the conflict. In addition, the written agreement serves as a record of what was decided in case future questions arise.

The peer mediator closes the session by shaking hands with the disputants, having the disputants shake hands, and thanking them for participating in mediation. These gestures symbolize mutual respect and promote cooperation.

1. ***Write the agreement reached by the disputants on the Peer Mediation Agreement form.***

2. ***Ask each disputant to sign the agreement. Then sign the agreement yourself.***

3. ***Shake hands with each person and congratulate the person for working to reach an agreement.***

4. ***Ask both of the disputants to shake hands.***

5. ***Close by saying, "Thank you for participating in mediation."***

Sample Peer Mediation Agreement

Peer mediator ___Rodney Anderson_____ Date __2/15/91___

Briefly describe the conflict: ___Andrew borrowed Heather's Walkman and took it into school_____

___even though Heather asked him not to do it. The principal confiscated the Walkman.___

_____

_____

_____

_____

Type of conflict (check one) ☐ Rumor ☐ Threat ☐ Name-calling ☐ Fighting
☑ Loss of property ☐ Other (specify) _____

The students whose signatures appear below met with a peer mediator and with the assistance of the mediator reached the following agreement.

Disputant ___Heather_____

Agrees to ___Act calmer and not yell at Andrew if a problem happens in the future.___

___She will talk with Andrew first to check things out and will not jump to conclusions.___

_____

Disputant ___Andrew_____

Agrees to ___Talk with the principal today to see if he can get Heather's Walkman. If he cannot,___

___he will ask if the principal will accept Andrew's Walkman in place of Heather's. Then___

___he will return Heather's Walkman to her.___

We have made and signed this agreement because we believe it resolves the issue(s) between us.

Andrew Smith	_Heather Jones_
Disputant signature	Disputant signature
Rodney Anderson	_15_
Peer mediator signature	Length of mediation (minutes)

Being a peer mediator is not always easy, but it is always a challenge. It is important to be positive and optimistic even though a mediation is difficult or the outcome is not as you expect. Remember, you are there only to offer your skilled assistance.

▲ ***The problem belongs to the disputants—they own it and are the only ones who can solve it.***

The times when mediations seem difficult or frustrating can become times of growth and change for everyone. Take the opportunity to talk with other peer mediators or adult staff members and share your thoughts and feelings.

▲ ***If there is honest communication, thinking will be expanded and boundaries will be broken.***

Encouraging another's efforts, sharing perspectives, and cooperating to solve human problems is a lifelong challenge. Through mutual support and respect, everyone will become stronger and better able to reach common goals.

▲ ***As Gandhi said, "If we are to reach real peace in this world, we shall have to begin teaching cooperation to the children."***

Caucusing is a strategy used in special situations to help disputants reach an agreement. Caucusing simply means meeting with each disputant individually. It may take place more than once and at any time during peer mediation, or it may not be used at all. It is the mediator's responsibility to decide whether or not a caucus is necessary.

REASONS FOR CAUCUSING

Caucusing can be used in a number of ways.

▲ To uncover information or clarify details that disputants may be willing to give only in private

▲ To move beyond an impasse

▲ To reduce tension between disputants

▲ To explore options

▲ To give people time to think alone and reflect

▲ To build trust in the peer mediator

GUIDELINES FOR CAUCUSING

1. **Give both disputants the opportunity to meet individually with you.**
   ("I want to meet with each of you alone.")

2. **During the individual meetings, use the procedures in Step 2 (gather information), Step 3 (focus on common interests), and Step 4 (create options), depending on the situation.**

3. **Before returning to the joint session, be sure you have a clear understanding of what information the disputants do not want revealed.**
   (All statements made during caucusing are confidential unless the disputant agrees that the information can be shared. "Everything said when we are alone is confidential. I will not share anything said with the other disputant unless you give me permission.")

4. **When both parties return to the joint session, summarize common interests and return to the step in the process where the disputants were when the caucus was called.**

You might think determining what is at the bottom of a conflict is an easy matter, but often what the conflict appears to be about is not the only issue involved. People sometimes have **hidden interests** in a conflict situation—and often these hidden interests are unmet basic needs for belonging, power, freedom, or fun.

As mentioned in the reading for Activity 3, conflicts that appear to be about **limited resources** or **different values** are often really about **unmet basic needs**. For example, suppose Robert is upset because his friend LaToya has not repaid some money she borrowed. In this case, you might think the conflict is caused by limited resources (in other words, a lack of money). But when LaToya offers to pay the money back in installments over a few weeks, Robert refuses to accept her solution. In reality, Robert may view LaToya's failure to repay the loan as a lack of respect and feel that his need for **power** is being threatened. The conflict is unlikely to be resolved until Robert's unmet need is recognized. In the mediation session, this recognition could come in the form of an apology from LaToya for not repaying the money as she had first promised.

Or suppose Maria is somebody who places a high value on honesty in friendships. She is angry with her friend Angela because Angela lied to her. In mediation, Maria will not accept Angela's explanations. Is the conflict the result of **different values** about honesty? Maybe yes and maybe no. In this case, Maria may be bothered less by the clash of values than by the fact that she feels she must cut herself off from Angela because Angela lied. In other words, Maria's need for **belonging** may be threatened. If this is the case, any solution to the problem will have to involve helping Maria decide whether she wants to accept Angela as a friend again.

An important part of your job as a peer mediator is to try to figure out what is really causing a conflict. If you do not, the agreements you help disputants reach are unlikely to be lasting ones.

Anger is a strong human emotion that is a signal that one or more of our basic needs (belonging, power, freedom, or fun) are not being met. Although most people think of anger as being a negative feeling, it is really neither good nor bad. The way people choose to process their anger can have either positive or negative outcomes, however.

One way to process anger is by ***turning it inward***. The person who behaves this way is often depressed. In addition, because he never expresses his anger, no one ever knows what he thinks or wants. As a result, he rarely gets his needs met.

Another way to process anger is ***aggression***. Being aggressive means verbally or physically attacking another individual. This includes fighting, yelling, name-calling, put-downs, and so forth. Generally, aggression turns people off, or they choose to react in a similarly aggressive way, and the problem just gets worse.

A third way to process anger is ***passive-aggression***. The person behaving this way looks calm on the outside but is really angry inside. She might show anger by rolling her eyes, interrupting, or refusing to cooperate. Others tend to avoid the passive-aggressive person or choose to get angry in return.

Still another way to process anger is ***assertion***. The assertive person knows he is angry and chooses to express that feeling in an appropriate way. He knows what he wants and needs and can ask for it without showing disrespect for other people's wants and needs. Dealing with anger by being assertive makes it much more likely that people will be able to cooperate and reach a mutually satisfying solution.

As a peer mediator, you can help people process their anger through assertion, not aggression or passive-aggression.

Think of the different types of students who go to your school. Think of their different backgrounds, values, and interests. We are all different—we are different sizes and have different color hair, eyes, and skin. We have different religions and biases. Unfortunately, people often react to these differences with prejudice. When we prejudge a person because of age, race, sex, disability, or social class, that is prejudice. Prejudice can cause discrimination and oppression, and it keeps people from meeting their basic needs.

Your ethnic background, income, where you live, and how you were brought up make up your **cultural background**. As a peer mediator, it is important for you to understand your own cultural background, biases, and behaviors. To be effective, you must become aware of how you view and interact with individuals who are different from you.

It is your role as a peer mediator to help disputants understand **individual differences**—this understanding is essential to finding common interests. Further, through your sensitivity, you can become a powerful model to help others learn to respect individual differences. This respect promotes cooperation and in turn makes resolution possible.

Peer Mediation Forms

Peer Mediation Request

Date _____

Names of students in conflict:

_____ Grade _____

_____ Grade _____

_____ Grade _____

_____ Grade _____

Where conflict occurred (check one)

☐ Bus   ☐ Classroom   ☐ Hallway   ☐ Cafeteria   ☐ Outdoors

☐ Other (specify) _____

Briefly describe the problem:

_____

_____

_____

_____

_____

_____

Mediation requested by (check one)

☐ Student   ☐ Teacher   ☐ Counselor   ☐ Administrator

☐ Other (specify) _____

Signature of person requesting mediation _____

Brainstorming Worksheet

List all the possible options.

▲ What could be done to resolve this dispute?

▲ What other possibilities can you think of?

▲ In the future, what could you do differently?

1. _____

2. _____

3. _____

4. _____

5. _____

6. _____

7. _____

8. _____

9. _____

10. _____

Peer Mediation Agreement

Peer mediator _____ Date _____

Briefly describe the conflict: _____

_____

_____

_____

_____

Type of conflict (check one) ☐ Rumor ☐ Threat ☐ Name-calling ☐ Fighting
☐ Loss of property ☐ Other (specify) _____

The students whose signatures appear below met with a peer mediator and with the assistance of the mediator reached the following agreement.

Disputant _____

Agrees to _____

_____

_____

Disputant _____

Agrees to _____

_____

_____

We have made and signed this agreement because we believe it resolves the issue(s) between us.

_____   _____
Disputant signature   Disputant signature

_____   _____
Peer mediator signature   Length of mediation (minutes)

Peer Mediator Contract

As a peer mediator, I understand my role is to help students resolve conflicts peacefully. As a peer mediator, I will do my best to respect the participants of mediation, remain neutral, and keep the mediation confidential.

As a peer mediator, I agree to the following terms.

▲ To complete all training sessions

▲ To maintain confidentiality in all mediations

▲ To responsibly conduct general duties of a peer mediator, including conducting mediations, completing all necessary forms, and promoting the program

▲ To maintain satisfactory school conduct (this includes requesting mediation before taking other action if I become involved in a conflict)

▲ To maintain satisfactory grades in all classes and make up any class work missed during training or mediation sessions

▲ To serve as a peer mediator until the end of the year

Possible actions if these responsibilities are not met are as follows.

▲ First time: Warning

▲ Second time: Loss of peer mediator status for 1 month

▲ Third time: Suspension as a peer mediator

I accept these responsibilities for the school year.

Student signature _____ Date _____

Glossary

ACTIVE LISTENING: Using nonverbal behaviors such as tone of voice, eye contact, and gestures to indicate understanding

AGGRESSION: Forceful action or attack

APOLOGIZE: To admit error or discourtesy by an expression of regret

ARBITRATE: To hear and decide a solution for two parties in controversy

ASSERTION: Expressing one's needs and wants in a way that shows respect for others' needs and wants

AVOID: To keep away from, stay clear of, shun

BASIC NEEDS: Needs that underlie all human behavior (belonging, power, freedom, fun)

BEHAVE: To act, function, or conduct oneself in a specific way

BELONGING: A feeling of being part of a group or in natural association with others (one of the four basic needs)

BIASED: Having a settled and often prejudiced outlook

BRAINSTORMING: A technique for helping disputants create as many options as they can for solving their problem

CAUCUS: Meeting with each disputant individually

CHOICE: Option or selection; power of deciding

CLARIFY: To make clearer or easier to understand

COMBINE: To bring into a state of unity, join, merge, or blend; to join forces for a common purpose or enter into an alliance

COMMUNICATE: To express thoughts, feelings, and actions so they are understood

COMMUNITY: A social group having common interests; similarity or identity among people

COMPROMISE: A settlement of differences in which each side makes concessions

CONFIDENTIAL: Private or secret

CONFLICT: Controversy or disagreement; to come into opposition

CONFRONT: To face with hostility or oppose defiantly

CONSEQUENCE: That which logically or naturally follows an action

CONTROL: To direct, guide, or influence

COOPERATION: Associating for mutual benefit; working toward a common end or purpose

CREATE: To bring into being, originate, or produce

CULTURAL BACKGROUND: A person's ethnic background, income, place of residence, and upbringing

DEESCALATE: To decrease the intensity of

DIFFERENCE: The condition or degree of being unlike, dissimilar, or diverse

DISAGREEMENT: A failure or refusal to agree; a difference of opinion

DISCRIMINATION: An act based on prejudice

DISPUTANT: One engaged in an argument or conflict

DIVERSITY: The fact or quality of being different or distinct

EMOTION: A strong feeling (for example, joy, sorrow, reverence, hate, love)

EMPATHIC: Characterized by understanding so intimate that the feelings, thoughts, and actions of one are easily known by another

ESCALATE: To increase or intensify

ETHNIC: Relating to large groups of people classed according to common racial, national, or cultural background

FREEDOM: The capacity to exercise choice or free will (one of the four basic needs)

FUN: Enjoyment, pleasure, amusement, playful behavior (one of the four basic needs)

GROUND RULE: One of several basic rules for conducting peer mediation, spelled out to disputants at the beginning of the session

HIDDEN INTEREST: In a conflict situation, a basic need or want that people may have that does not appear on the surface to be related to the problem

HOSTILITY: State of being antagonistic; hatred

INTEREST: Involvement or concern; the aspect of something that enables it to matter

INTOLERANCE: Quality or condition of being unable to grant equal freedom of expression; bigotry

MEDIATE: To intervene between two or more disputing parties in order to bring about an agreement

MISUNDERSTANDING: A failure to understand; a disagreement

NEGOTIATE: To discuss with another or others in order to come to terms or reach an agreement

OPTION: Something that may be chosen; an alternative course of action

PASSIVE-AGGRESSION: An indirect expression of one's anger (for example, by refusing to cooperate)

PEER MEDIATION: A process of conflict resolution in which students work together to solve their own problems

PERCEPTION: The process or act of insight, intuition, or knowledge gained through the senses

POSITION: A mental posture or point of view

POWER: The ability to act or perform effectively (one of the four basic needs)

PREJUDICE: An adverse judgment or opinion formed without knowledge or examination of facts; irrational suspicion or hatred for a particular group, race, or religion; the holding of preconceived judgments

59

RECONCILE: To reestablish friendship between; to settle or resolve

RESOLUTION: A course of action decided upon to solve a problem

RESOURCE: An available supply that can be drawn upon when needed

RESPECT: To feel or show esteem for; to honor

RESPONSIBILITY: Personal accountability or the ability to act without guidance

STEREOTYPE: A mental picture that reflects an oversimplified judgment about something or someone

SUMMARIZE: To restate in a brief, concise form

SYNERGY: Action of two or more people working together to achieve something neither could alone

TRUST: To have confidence in or feel sure of; faith

UNDERSTAND: To perceive and comprehend the nature and significance of; to know and be tolerant or sympathetic toward

VALUE: A principle, standard, or quality considered worthwhile or desirable; to regard highly

VIOLENCE: The abusive or unjust exercise of power; physical force exerted for the purpose of violating, damaging, or abusing